Hey, God! What is America?

Roxie Cawood Gibson

Printed and Illustrated by James C. Gibson

Home Inc.
Publishing

First Printing - 1981
Second Printing - 1994

ISBN   0-9640392-6-5

This book is
dedicated
with utmost love
to
our Lord and Saviour,
Jesus Christ.

This one's for
<u>You</u>,
Paul Harvey !

Hey, God !
What is
America ?

Hey, God! What is America anyway?

I know what it used to be, but somehow, God, I think it's changed a little bit.

I know how proud I always am to stand tall and straight and put my right hand over my heart and say, "I pledge allegiance to the flag of the United States of America and to the Republic for which it stands". But not very many people even say the pledge any more... do you think it's because they don't know what it means, God?

I wish they would teach us about it at school..... we don't talk about America very much at school, maybe it's because the teachers think we learn about it at home.

But then,

we don't talk much
about America at home
either.... maybe it's
because our moms and
dads think we learn
about it at school.
Somewhere along the
line we got confused
about who teaches
who what, didn't
we, God?

Anyway, to be honest with You, God, I wasn't sure I understood what the pledge meant so I looked in the dictionary to see what the word allegiance means and it says, "The duty of being loyal to one's ruler, government or country. Well, you don't have to be an Einstein to figure that out do you, God? How many of us are really loyal to our government?

8

Now, I'm just a kid and grown-ups don't think I pay any attention to what they're saying, so you'd be surprised at the things I hear them say about politics (You aren't really surprised, God, 'cause You hear them too).

You know, God, some people think You only hear them on Sunday in church, They think You aren't listening the rest of the week.

Boy, oh, boy! Are they going to be surprised some day when they find out You have heard EVERYTHING! You know God, sometimes little people are smarter

than big people, but
don't you tell them we
know this, ok, God?

Well, anyway, back to
the pledge -- " I pledge
allegiance to the flag
of the United States of
America and to the
Republic for which it
stands. One nation under
God...." -- Uh-oh, God,
here's the next problem.
I don't even have to
go to the dictionary
for this one.

" ONE NATION UNDER
GOD . . . . . . "

We _have_ forgotten that
we're under You, haven't
we, God?

Why, God, they even say it's ~~uncosti~~ ~~unconstin~~ unconstutual (Oh, You know what I mean, God) to talk out loud to You at school. Now that really makes me mad, 'cause I can talk out loud to my other friends and You are the best friend I have, so why can't I talk out loud to You, God?

You just help me and when I grow up we'll do something about this. I think it's about time someone did!

Okay, here we go again.

"I pledge allegiance to the flag of the United States of America and to the Republic for which it stands, one nation under God, indivisible, with liberty and justice for all." Well, back to the dictionary. By the way, God, do You know Mr. Webster ....

Well of course You do.
You know everyone, don't
You, God? The problem
is that everyone doesn't
know You!

Well, anyway, Mr. Webster
must have really been
smart to know the
meaning of all those
words! And he says
indivisible means
can't be separated. I've
thought a lot about
this, God, and I can
remember some times
when everyone in our

country seemed close to each other and not separated.

CAN'T BE SEPARATED!

Just like we were one big family!

It was times like when we were having hurricanes, floods, earthquakes or other bad things like tornadoes. We were all united and praying for the same cause. So maybe we are getting back on the right track.

23

I've been trying to figure out how we got off the track, God, and I think it was because we forgot to listen to You. Now I don't know how this happened, and so far I haven't found who does. When I ask someone about it, they just mumble and say we'll talk about it later.

24

Now, You know what they
mean when they say
"later" don't you, God?
That means they don't
know the answer.
Do You know why we
pay people not to work,
God? Well, it really
doesn't matter why we
started it, because one
of the greatest things
about America is that

when we make mistakes
we can do something
about them. And I
think we are trying to
do something about our
mistakes now.

You know, God, I love
America so much I just
want to help everyone
love it. I want to fly
the flag, but I'm afraid
if I do someone will
stop and want to buy
some postage stamps,
'cause about the only
place I see the flag
flying any more is at
the Post Office and the
government buildings.
I think it would help if
we all started being

"flag wavers", don't you?

We should all be proud of our land --- our mountains, valleys, lakes and streams and seas.

But most of all, God, in America You have given us freedom and the right to be anything we want to be .....
a doctor, lawyer, teacher, scientist, writer, news commentator, farmer, truck driver or whatever else we would like to be! So I sure am proud to

be an American!
Thanks, God, for letting
me live here!

You have given us so
much, God, that we have
gotten greedy with it.
I don't like the word
"greedy" since I found
out that it means

"wanting more than one
needs or deserves"
(Thank you again,
  Mr. Webster). I hate
to tell you this, but I
don't like the word
"greedy" because it
describes me, and

greed spreads faster
than crabgrass and
chokes out everything
it touches.

You see, it starts in little ways of wanting more. If my friend has a new bicycle, then I want one. If he has a horse, then I want one. If he has a swimming pool, then I want one. If he gets to go on a vacation trip, then I want to go on one too. If he had a rattlesnake, I'd probably want one too....

and am I afraid
of snakes!

Anyway, I get so busy
spending my time wanting
that I don't have time to
be thankful for what I
have. I had just about
forgotten how much fun
it is to climb a tree,
take a walk, play in the
creek or just lie under
the shade of the tree
and think about the
world of "make-believe."
I think we live in the
world of "make believe"
now because the other
day I heard my Dad

say that sooner or later someone was going to have to pay the piper. Now that sounds like "make-believe" to me, so I asked him what he was talking about. He said that after you dance to the piper's music, the piper has to be paid. Sometimes grown-up talk doesn't make much sense to me, God.

I hated to ask my Dad
about it again because
sometimes he calls me
"Question Box". You don't
think my name is Question
Box, do You, God?

You know, God, You're the
only one I can depend
on to help me when
everyone else gets tired
of answering my
questions. Come to think
of it, God, You're the

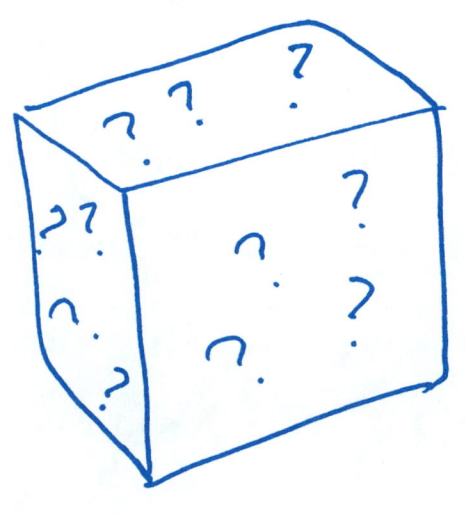

only one with all
the right answers
too!

Well, anyway, back to Dad.
He explained to me that
we had all been wasteful
with water, air, gas,
food and oil, and
now we will have
to pay the piper!
We won't have as much
of these in the
future, and they will
cost us more!

Now that makes
sense!

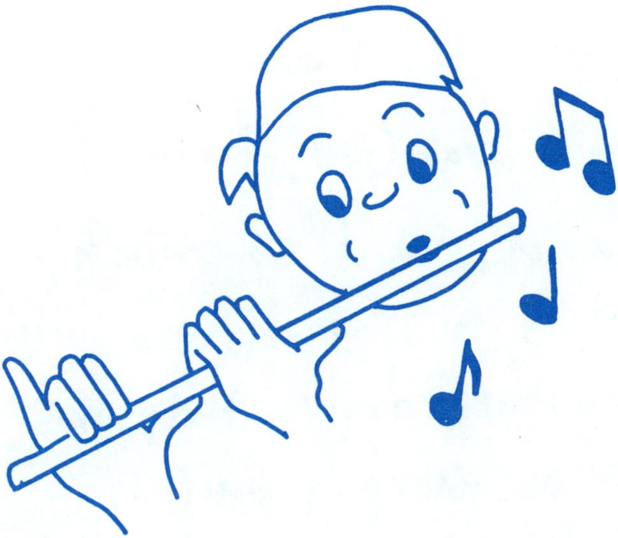

So, God, if America has changed it's because we have changed. We've been wasteful and ungrateful and greedy. So, dear God, help me to not want so much, then maybe others will do the same. Help me to be more proud of America and to fly its flag every day. Start with me, God. Help me to want less and care for others more.

I think that's what
You've been trying to
tell me, but you see,
God, I talk more than
I listen so I guess
I didn't hear You.
So, dear God, help me
to stand tall and proud
for my country. Help me
tell others that we
should be one nation
under God. And, God,
let all of us have
little goose bumps on

44

our arms and sometimes a tiny tear of joy in our eyes as we stand united and say,

"I pledge allegiance to the flag of the United States of America".

Thanks God, and remember I love You!

OTHER BOOKS BY ROXIE GIBSON

HEY, GOD, LISTEN!

HEY, GOD, WHERE ARE YOU?

HEY, GOD, WHAT IS CHRISTMAS?

HEY, GOD, HURRY!

HEY, GOD WHAT IS DEATH?

***

TWO LITTLE FISHES AND FIVE
    LOAVES OF BREAD

JUST ME, LORD

DO RAGWEEDS BLOOM?